OLD SCHOOL

AMERICA

*511 Reflections on the
Traditional and Patriotic Values
that Best Define America*

Peter Slovenski, Patrick Vardaro,
and Richard Sherman

Ray Jacqmin, illustrator

TowleHouse Publishing
Hendersonville, Tennessee

TowleHouse books are distributed by National Book Network (NBN),
4720 Boston Way, Lanham, Maryland 20706.

Library of Congress Cataloging-in-Publication data is available.
ISBN: 1-931249-29-6

Cover design by Gore Studio, Inc.
Page design by Mike Towle

Printed in the United States of America
1 2 3 4 5 6 — 08 07 06 05 04

Contents

INTRODUCTION

The old school teaches the wisdom of the ages. It describes a way of life that reached its cultural peak in America between 1900 and 1967. The old school teaches a way of living that emphasizes honor, hard work, romance, loyalty, patriotism, courage, religion, education, and doing what is best for everyone and the future of the nation.

Old school America has a reverence for the past, and for the trials and tribulations that carried our ancestors forward. The old school is forever getting smarter and better by comparing various ways of doing things and eventually uniting behind the best ideas and turning them into traditions. Here are some old school cultural standards that were admired in America from 1900 to 1967. They are standards we can still learn from today.

1

THE ESSENCE OF OLD SCHOOL AMERICA

"AND SO, MY FELLOW AMERICANS, ASK NOT
WHAT YOUR COUNTRY CAN DO FOR YOU; ASK
WHAT YOU CAN DO FOR YOUR COUNTRY."

—John F. Kennedy

———————————————

Doing chores without getting
an allowance is old school.

———

Reciting the Pledge of Allegiance
in class is old school.

———

"Sticks and stones will break my
bones, but names will never
hurt me" is old school.

———

Being generous to others but thrifty
for yourself is old school.

———

2

Benjamin Franklin was old school.

———

Self-reliance, self-sufficiency,
self-confidence, and self-discipline
are all old school. Self-esteem is
not old school. The old school
teaches a person to esteem
things other than one's self.

———

Keeping a diary or
a journal is old school.

———

"All men are created equal"
is old school.

———

"Equal pay for an equal day's work"
is old school.

———

In the old school,
parents backed
up the teachers
100 percent of the time.
In the old school, the
parents and teachers
were on the same side,
and the children were
well educated by
this team.

2

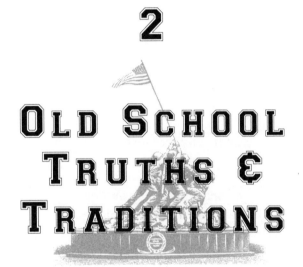

OLD SCHOOL
TRUTHS &
TRADITIONS

*T*he old school prides itself on retaining traditions and staying the same; but the old school also prides itself on the most brilliant search for truth that history has ever known. The search for truth leads the old school to improve, evolve, and move forward.

Queen Elizabeth is old school.

George Washington Carver
was old school.

King Arthur was old school.

Susan B. Anthony was old school.

John Glenn is old school.

Thomas Edison was old school.

———

The Wright Brothers
were old school.

———

Marconi was old school.

———

William Tyndale was old school.

———

Respecting culture from
the past and respecting crazy
old relatives—even when you
don't agree with them—is old school.

———

The Golden Rule is old school.

———

Being honest to others
and with yourself is old school.

———

Amelia Earhart was old school.

Nikola Tesla was old school.

The August 1963 civil rights
march on Washington
was an old school march.

The Polish Solidarity
movement was old school.

Religions are old school because they
are usually devoted to finding and
preserving eternal truths.

Harry Truman was old school.

3

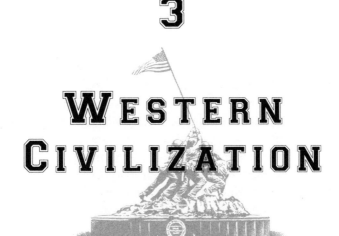

WESTERN
CIVILIZATION

The old school was proud of Western civilization. The old school was proud of the achievements of Western civilization, which include democracy, capitalism, freedom of the press, unsurpassed equality of races and genders, freedom of religion, separation of church and state, and free public school education.

Western civilization allows and even encourages the most incredibly high levels of criticism and examination of itself. Western civilization is not afraid of comparison to any other civilization because the very genius of Western civilization is that if something works better than what we are doing now, Western civilization will study, embrace, and then absorb it.

The old school took pride in building and improving the tradition using ideas and contributions from within as well as from the outside. The old school gave a lot of credit to the intelligence of the tradition without caring what race or gender came up with our constitution or numbering system.

10

It has become fashionable to emphasize that Western civilization has oppressed some people. The old school recognized that it is Western civilization—not any other civilization that originated in Asia, Africa, or South America—that has created the greatest levels of racial equality and the greatest equality that women have ever known in the history of the world. Western civilization doesn't attract so many immigrants because it oppresses people; it attracts so many immigrants because it FREES people. The old school understood this was a civilization that could withstand honest examination; but it also understood that Western civilization is a precious creation to be loved and to be defended from cheap and persistent criticism.

Winston Churchill was old school.

———

Franklin Delano Roosevelt
was old school.

———

"Ask not what your country can do
for you; ask what you can do for
your country" is old school.

———

Dwight D. Eisenhower was old school.

———

The "melting pot" idea is old school.

———

Politicians' writing their own
speeches is old school.

———

The Protestant work
ethic is old school.

———

People with real jobs being elected to office is old school. Making a career out of politics is not old school.

———

Great oratory such as the Gettysburg Address and "Fireside Chats" with FDR are old school.

———

Seeking solutions in private enterprise or community institutions first is old school.

———

Thomas Jefferson is old school. He said: "I believe in a government lean and frugal."

———

Local government is old school.

———

Going on strike and marching
in demonstrations to change
CORPORATE policies is old school.
Voting in elections to change
government policies is old school.
Writing letters to change
government policies is old school.
Marching in protest to change
government policies when you cannot
vote is old school, but marching to
protest government policies when
you can vote is not old school.

———

Christmas carols are old school.

———

"The Star Spangled Banner," "God
Bless America," "My Country 'Tis of
Thee," and "The Battle Hymn of the
Republic" are old school.

———

14

"Taps" is old school.

———

Famous quotations and
platitudes are old school.

—

"The Midnight Ride of
Paul Revere" is old school.

—

The Federalist Papers are old school.

—

Big Ben is old school.

—

The Eiffel Tower is old school.

—

The Empire State Building
is old school.

—

Buildings covered in ivy are old school.

———

Lighthouses are old school.

The Golden Gate Bridge and the
Brooklyn Bridge are old school.

———

The London Bridge was
old school, until it got sold.

———

Profiles in Courage by
John F. Kennedy is old school.

———

The Lincoln Memorial is old school.

———

Buildings with columns in
the front are old school.

———

The classics are old school.

———

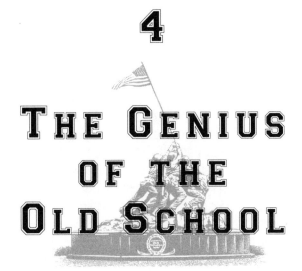

4

THE GENIUS OF THE OLD SCHOOL

"THERE IS NO ROOM IN THIS COUNTRY FOR
HYPHENATED AMERICANISM.. . . THE ONE
ABSOLUTELY CERTAIN WAY OF BRINGING
THIS NATION TO RUIN, OF PREVENTING ALL
POSSIBILITY OF ITS CONTINUING TO BE A
NATION AT ALL, WOULD BE TO PERMIT IT
TO BECOME A TANGLE OF SQUABBLING
NATIONALITIES."

—**Theodore Roosevelt**, *New York City,*
October 12, 1915

The Genius of the Old School

*T*he old school recognizes that the
original and most profound genius of the
United States is the melting pot. Never before
or since has any culture brought so many
diverse peoples together and then inspired
them to become united. People of different
religions live in the same neighborhoods, and
interracial marriage is common. E Pluribus
Unum is old school. E Pluribus Plures is
not. English immersion in public schools is
old school because the beginning of unity is
a common language. Bilingual education in
public schools is not old school. People
immigrate to the United States from Italy,
China, Iran, and Somalia not to remain
European, Asian, Persian, or African, but to
become American. They bring ideas and
traditions to America that are either
integrated into the cultural alloy or
discarded. The melting pot that includes
influence from all continents is old school.

"I HAVE A DREAM THAT MY FOUR LITTLE
CHILDREN WILL ONE DAY LIVE IN A NATION
WHERE THEY WILL NOT BE JUDGED BY
THE COLOR OF THEIR SKIN, BUT BY THE
CONTENT OF THEIR CHARACTER."

—**Rev. Martin Luther King**, *who was old school*

J. C. Watts is old school.

Judging people by the content
of their character and not by the
color of their skin is old school.

Democracy in America by
Alexis de Toqueville is old school.

The Statue of Liberty is old school.

The Genius of the Old School

Ellis Island is old school.

———◆———

Little Italy, Chinatown, and ethnic
neighborhoods where immigrants
first congregate in neighborhoods
before moving out into the
melting pot are old school.

———◆———

Interethnic marriage and
interracial marriage are old school.

———◆———

Legal immigration is old school.
Illegal immigration is not old school.

———◆———

Loyalty to your own family or
ethnic group is old school; but
bias against any other ethnic
group is not old school.

———◆———

Favoring anyone for the color
of their skin is not old school.

The Morse Code is old school.

Polkas are old school.

Bed & breakfast inns are old school.

The space race was old school.

Beef stew is old school.

Newspapers are old school.

The Great Wall of
China is old school.

———

The Pyramids are old school.

———

Fallout shelters are old school.

———

Encyclopedias are old school.

———

The old school knew that the
Republic was only as strong as
the character of its citizenry.
In the old school, the first
purpose of education was to
strengthen a child's character.

———

Theodore Roosevelt was old school.

———

Colin Powell is old school.

———

Concerts on the town
common are old school.

———

Town meetings are old school.

———

Church soup kitchens and
food pantries are old school.

———

Forwarding e-mail is not old school.

———

5

OLD SCHOOL
POP CULTURE

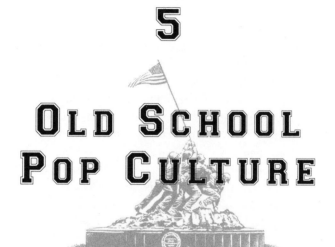

O ld School pop culture attempted to reflect the best of society. If art is truly educational, inspiring, and enlightening, then adults must promote good standards through the majority of the art comprising popular culture. If you want people to have manners, then you show people using manners in movies, books, music, and television. If you want people to make commitments to marriage and raising children, then pop culture should show that in a positive, artistic way.

Old school popular culture had to sell within cultural standards that supported the kind of world in which people could raise children, and children could safely walk the streets. The best accomplishments of popular culture—Camelot, Rhapsody in Blue, or The Wizard of Oz—were both artistically popular and artistically inspirational. You could not make a success of any contribution to pop culture if it encouraged anti-social behavior such as treating women as sexual objects or violence toward police officers.

Movies without swearing are old school.

Jimmy Stewart was old school.

All books that were made into
Walt Disney movies are old school.

Katharine Hepburn was old school.

Movie theaters with
balconies are old school.

Tom Hanks is old school.

In the old school, people went
to drive-in restaurants instead
of drive-thru restaurants.

The Madeline books are old school.

———

Double features are old school.

———

Nancy Drew books are old school.

———

The Bobsey Twins are old school.

———

The Hardy Boys are old school.

———

Black & white movies are old school.

———

In the old school, movies didn't need ratings because they were all clean.

———

Shirley Temple was old school.

———

Rosemary Clooney was old school.

———

Tchaikovsky was old school.

———

John Philip Sousa's
music is old school.

———

Jukeboxes are old school.

———

Country music
tends to be old school.

———

Pianos are old school.

———

Harmonicas are old school.

———

The Beach Boys sounded
old school but did things
that weren't old school.

———

Louis Armstrong was old school.

———

George Burns was old school.

———

Frank Sinatra sounded old
school, and pretended to be old
school, but he was faux old school.

———

Nat King Cole was old school.

———

Glenn Miller was old school.

———

Radio programs are old school.

———

Telegrams are old school.

———

Record players are old school.

———

Jazz, big bands, and
cornets are old school.

———

Acoustic guitars are old school.

———

Rabbit-eared televisions are old school.

The Beatles started off old school.

———

Folk music is old school.

———

In the old school, it
was a treat to watch TV.

———

Yo-yos are old school.

———

Hula-Hoops are old school.

———

<u>The Ed Sullivan Show</u> was old school.

———

The Flintstones are old school.

———

<u>The Dick Van Dyke Show</u>
was old school.

———•———

Mary Tyler Moore is old school.

———•———

Jack Benny was old school.

———•———

<u>Bonanza</u> was old school.

———•———

Saturday-morning
cartoons are old school.

———•———

Any show in which the
parents give good advice
to their children is old school.

———•———

<u>Leave it to Beaver</u> was old school.

Old School Pop Culture

Root beer floats are old school.

———

Zorro is old school.

———

The Lone Ranger is old school.

———

Batman is old school.

———

Superman is old school.

———

Superheroes are
pretty much all old school.

———

<u>Boy's Life</u> is old school.

———

Reader's Digest is old school.

—•—

Good Housekeeping is old school.

—•—

The Farmer's Almanac
is old school.

—•—

Drive-in theaters are old school.

—•—

Ozzie and Harriet were old school.

—•—

The Music Man is old school.

—•—

The Sound of Music is old school.

—•—

<u>Goodnight Moon</u> is old school.

———◦———

Waltzes are old school.

———◦———

The Twist is old school.

———◦———

<u>The Wizard of Oz</u> is old school.

———◦———

Peter Pan is old school.

———◦———

<u>The Three Stooges</u>
is old school.

———◦———

The Brothers Grimm are old school.

———◦———

Winnie the Pooh is old school.

———•———

Charlie Brown is old school.

———•———

Spaghetti westerns
are old school.

———•———

Lassie is old school.

———•———

Dick Tracy is old school.

———•———

Mother Goose is old school.

———•———

Card games such as bridge, wist,
hearts, and cribbage are old school.

———•———

Norman Rockwell paintings are old school.

Flat-top haircuts are old school.

G.I. Joe is old school.

Steak and eggs are old school.

S'mores are old school.

Pogo sticks are old school.

Tarzan was old school.

Raggedy Ann is old school.

Dance marathons are old school.

Captain Kangaroo was old school.

6

OLD SCHOOL LIBERAL ARTS

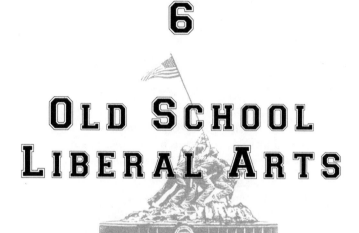

*F*ree public education taught a person how to live a successful life. Through literature, math, art, science, geography, history, spelling, and writing the old school taught every American child how to be self-reliant and how to recognize truth. Children studied a core curriculum that emphasized classics of Western tradition, along with reading, writing, and arithmetic. The idea of this free public liberal arts education was to educate children so they could grow up to be intelligent members of a free society. The old school had confidence that people were smart.

In the old school, the curriculum of literature and history in particular taught students that a united people had the power to be self-reliant and intelligent enough to make a success of themselves. The old school required roughly four things: an education, hard work, common sense, and not making babies until you were ready to raise them. An American liberal arts education rose to be the highest level of education in the world.

"READING IS TO THE MIND WHAT EXERCISE
IS TO THE BODY."

—Joseph Addison

———————————————

Robert Frost is old school.

———

Emily Dickinson is old school.

———

Herman Melville is old school.

———

Mark Twain was on the
cutting edge of the old school.

———

F. Scott Fitzgerald was on
the cutting edge of the
new school. Too much money
and drinking for the old school.

———

Dictionaries are old school.

———

The Bronte sisters are old school.

———

Wordsworth is old school.

———

Tennyson is old school.

———

Steinbeck is old school.

———

Hemingway characters try to be
old school, but sometimes they slip.

———

Sherlock Holmes is old school.

———

The Jim Corbett books about hunting
man-eating tigers are old school.

———

Jane Austen was old school.

———

<u>Wuthering Heights</u> is old school.

———

<u>Jane Eyre</u> is old school.

———

Latin and Greek are old school.

Writing letters is old school.

Colleges & universities used to be
old school, but they are not anymore.

—◦—

<u>War and Peace</u> is old school.

—◦—

<u>Gone With the Wind</u> is old school.

—◦—

<u>The Secret Garden</u> is old school.

—◦—

Charles Dickens is old school.

—◦—

<u>Robinson Crusoe</u> is old school.

—◦—

<u>GE College Bowl</u>
was old school.

—◦—

Writing for your school
newspaper is old school.

———

"Wisdom is more valuable
than gold" is old school.

———

Science research is old
school, but social science
research is not old school.

———

Striving to do
your best is old school.

———

West Point is old school.

———

Annapolis is old school.

———

Looking up words in the dictionary is old school.

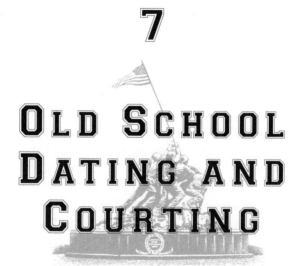

7

OLD SCHOOL
DATING AND
COURTING

*O*ld school songs were about love, not sex. The romance of two people in the old school was based on love and friendship; physical attraction was repressed unless love and friendship were present. As you fell in love with someone for the person they were, physical attraction was allowed to follow.

Men and women or boys and girls were taught to get to know each other through dating. Dating required men and women to learn how to behave around each other, and to relate to each other in intellectual and emotional terms. Dating was supposed to be fun, but also formal. In the old school, men and women recognized that a successful romance depended more on BEING the right person than finding the right person.

The system of courting and dating was responsible for producing the long-lasting and happy marriages that defined the old school. It was a grueling process designed to weed out men and women who would not make good spouses. In the old school, *marriage was a commitment "till death do us part." Men and women who were courting or engaged never lived together until they got married. While it is difficult to be apart from someone you love, it is important to test the strength of your love. Absence and abstinence make the heart grow fonder. If your love is real then it will transcend the hardship of being apart, and in fact it will gain strength from the discipline of your engagement.*

Writing love letters is old school.

Dating is old school.

Boys coming in the house
to speak with the parents
before a date is old school.

Getting a milkshake
with two straws is old school.

Having dinner with the parents
of your girlfriend is old school.

⸺

Not living together until
you get married is old school.

⸺

Making out at
Inspiration Point is old school.

⸺

Surprising your girlfriend
with flowers is old school.

⸺

Opening doors and holding chairs
for your girlfriend is old school.

⸺

Inexpensive weddings
are old school.

———

Inexpensive proms are old school.

———

Wearing your grandfather's
old watch on a chain or your
grandmother's engagement
ring is old school.

———

Letter sweaters are old school.

———

Writing thank-you
letters is old school.

———

Popcorn is old school.

———

Banana splits are old school.

———•———

Loafers are old school.

———•———

Narrow ties are old school.

———•———

Asking your girlfriend's
parents for permission to
marry their daughter is old school.

———•———

Cardigan sweaters are old school.

———•———

Holding hands is old school.

———•———

Sadie Hawkins dances
are old school.

———•———

Corsages are old school.

———

Pillbox hats are old school.

———

Bow ties are old school.

———

Scarves are old school.

———

Anything wool is old school.

———

Handkerchiefs are old school.

———

Suspenders are old school.

———

8

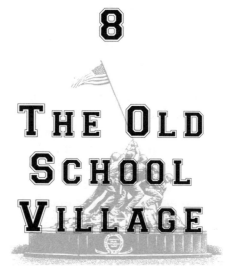

THE OLD
SCHOOL
VILLAGE

It takes an old school village to raise a child. Having a village raise a child is old school. If some boys were riding on a bus and used foul language in 1960, an adult on the bus would tell them to stop it. And the boys would usually stop for fear that the adult would tell their parents. All the adults in a community helped teach children manners and helped teach children how to behave in public so they would not embarrass their parents. Parents, teachers, and police officers were all on the same side working together to raise children to be courteous and show good character. All that instruction provided by the adults of a village was free public education.

Each town having its
own high school is old school.

Having your best friend
live next door is old school.

The Old School Village

Orphanages are old school.

———

Homecoming is old school.

———

Pep rallies are old school.

———

Going home for lunch is old school.

———

Neighborhood cookouts
are old school.

———

Old school teacher-to-student
ratios averaged 1-to-30
with little or no behavioral troubles.

———

Whole milk is old school.

———

Having fruit for
dessert is old school.

—◆—

Overcooked vegetables
are old school.

—◆—

Cabbage, turnips, beets,
spinach, peas in the pod,
and squash are old school.

—◆—

Beans-and-franks
dinners are old school.

—◆—

Public speaking is old school.

—◆—

Yard work is old school.

—◆—

Neighborhoods
safe enough to
leave the house
unlocked are old
school.

White picket
fences are old school.

———

Adults' correcting the
grammar of children is old school.

———

Going places where everyone
knows your name is old school.

———

Red and white checkerboard
tablecloths are old school.

———

"Please," "Thank You," and
"You're Welcome" are old school.

———

A doctor's house
call is old school.

———

The Old School Village

Weather vanes are old school.

———

Circuses, carnivals, and
state fairs are old school.

———

A napkin in the lap is old school.

———

"Yes, ma'am"; "No ma'am"; "Yes, sir";
"No, sir," are old school.

———

Family-sized tents made
of canvas and held up by a
big center pole are old school.

———

In the old school, manners
madeth the man or woman.

———

Climbing trees is old school.

———◆———

Taking hats off inside
buildings is old school.

———◆———

Hide-and-seek is old school.

———◆———

Rope swings and tire
swings are old school.

———◆———

Building forts is old school.

———◆———

Jigsaw puzzles are old school.

———◆———

Running through
backyard sprinklers on
a hot summer day is old school.

———◆———

9

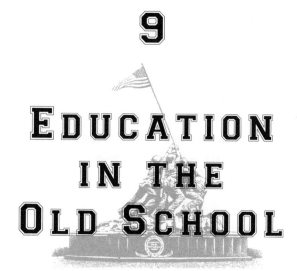

EDUCATION
IN THE
OLD SCHOOL

*N*ew schools emphasize cooperation, group projects, concepts, critical thinking, discussion, and student ideas. Girls dominate the honor roll in new schools; boys dominate the detention halls.

Old schools emphasized competition, self-discipline, content, lecture, and teacher direction. Boys and girls were roughly even on the honor rolls, and there were few boys who could not learn to behave and learn in regular classes. Boys still dominated the detention halls.

Memorization of multiplication tables is old school.

Good spelling and grammar are old school.

Arithmetic is old school.

Hot cereals (grits, cream of wheat, oatmeal, Maypo, etc.) are old school.

———•———

A thermos is old school.

———•———

The old school recognized
that the most important teachers
children had were their parents.

———•———

School assemblies are old school.

———•———

Spelling bees are old school.

———•———

Recess on the
playground is old school.

———•———

The study of
geography is old school.

Education in the Old School

Being disciplined by
your teacher is old school.

———

High school proms in the
school gymnasium are old school.

———

In the old school, parents
were responsible for getting
their children ready for
school, and then they were
also responsible for their behavior.

———

K-8 schools are old school.
Middle schools are not old school.

———

Pencil sharpeners are old school.

———

Going to school in either
a dress or a tie is old school.

———

Bedford Falls is old school.
Pottersville is not.

———

Instruction in
penmanship is old school.

———

Group projects are not old school.

———

Hopscotch is old school.

———

Scraping your knees is old school.

———

Education in the Old School

Off the wall and
four square are old school.

———

Mary Poppins is an old school teacher.

———

Science fairs are old school.

———

Paul Harvey is old school.

———

Boarding schools
tend to still be old school.

———

Studious people, sometimes
called nerds, are old school.

———

School
musicals
are old
school.

10

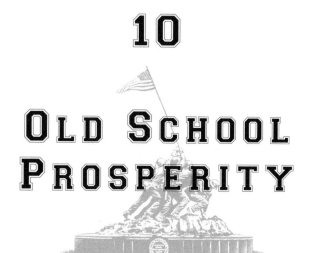

OLD SCHOOL PROSPERITY

When prosperity arrived in America following World War II, the old school generations often voted against new schools and new libraries EVEN WHEN THEY HAD THE MONEY to build them. Those generations believed the most important lessons could be taught for free and were better taught without fancy classrooms and fancy equipment. You could learn reading, writing, arithmetic, manners, common sense, and honor in an old school room or in an old library. Fancy buildings did not improve an old school education. Fancy buildings actually taught the wrong lesson.

The old school Latin phrase: *crescit sub pondere virtus*—means virtue increases under every hardship.

Keeping your day job while dreaming of a better future at night is old school.

Old School Prosperity

Delis are old school.

Boardwalks are old school.

Towns that have no interstates or
four-lane highways running through
them are often old school towns.

Farming is old school.

Furnaces are old school.

Downtowns are old school.

Barbershops with a red, white, &
blue pole in front are old school.

Hard work is old school.

Old School Prosperity

Doing things that don't
cost much money is old school.

———

Being hungry every
now and then is old school.

———

Growing your own fruits
and vegetables is old school.

———

Ice-cream parlors and
soda jerks are old school.

———

Getting your shoes
shined is old school.

———

Scrap metal is old school.

———

Lemonade stands are old school.

———

Gambling is not old school.

Manual labor is old school.

———•———

Returning bottles and
cans for money is old school.

———•———

The butcher, the baker, and the
candlestick maker are all old school.

———•———

Diners are old school.

———•———

Meat loaf is old school.

———•———

Potatoes are old school.

———•———

Angel food cake is old school.

———•———

"The harder you work, the
luckier you get" is old school.

———

Candy apples are old school.

———

Pretzels are old school.

———

Hot-dog stands are old school.

———

Breadboxes are old school.

———

Kellogg's Corn Flakes
are old school.

———

Wheaties are old school.

———

"Saving is a greater art
than earning" is old school.

American ingenuity is old school.

———•———

Apple pie is old school.

———•———

Brownies are old school.

———•———

Popsicles homemade in
ice-cube trays are old school.

———•———

Three square meals
a day are old school.

———•———

Saying grace before
supper is old school.

———•———

Glass milk bottles are old school.

———•———

Old School Prosperity

Jobs that involve walking,
such as policeman, mailman,
or caddie, are old school jobs.

———

Neighborhood stores are old school.

———

Piggy banks are old school.

———

Your mother sending you next
door to borrow an egg is old school.

———

Coupons are old school.

———

Attending night school while working
during the day is old school.

———

Paying with cash is old school.

———

11

OLD SCHOOL CONSERVATION

*E*nvironmentalism is old school. The old school has a fundamental preference for preserving the old and defending what is good. In the old school people only bought what they were going to use, and they were resourceful in how they used and recycled it. There wasn't much packaging on products sold in old school stores. In the old school, if you were cold in your house, you put on a sweater instead of turning up the thermostat. The old school principle of conservation is closely related to the old school principle of thriftiness.

Riding public transportation is old school, and common courtesy made it a pleasant experience. Sprawl is not old school. The only people who lived in the country were people who worked in the country. People who worked in town generally lived in town.

Preserving forests, rivers, lakes, clean air, and wildlife habitat is old school. In 1908, Theodore Roosevelt said conservation is "the chief material question that confronts us, second *only and second always to the great fundamental question of morality."*

Old school traditions that began with groups such as the Boy Scouts and Girl Scouts had a deep respect and reverence for nature. They were primarily interested in the moral development of children, which was linked to living in harmony with nature. Americans dumped raw sewage into rivers in 1950 because they didn't realize that harm was being done. When the harm was recognized and understood, it was old school scientists and civil servants (in the 1970s) who began to design and build sewage treatment plants. Greedy businessmen resisted the change. Girl Scouts are old school. Boy Scouts are old school. Fishermen are old school. Greedy businessmen are not old school.

Train travel is old school.

———

Walking to places is old school.

———

Roadside vegetable
stands are old school.

———

Slow highways and
fast trains are old school.

———

Giving up your seat on
a bus or train is old school.

———

Driving within the
speed limit is old school.

———

The Grand Canyon is old school.

———

National parks, state parks, county parks, and town parks are old school.

———

Chopping wood is old school.

———

Family farms are old school.

———

Two-lane highways are old school.

———

Telling your children, "Turn off the lights. We don't have stock in the power company," is old school.

———

Manual lawnmowers are old school.

———

Front porches are old school.

———

Brick buildings are old school.

Old School Conservation

In the old school,
you knew your neighbors.

———•———

Bird feeders are old school.

———•———

"There's no place
like home" is old school.

———•———

Handsaws, hammers,
and sandpaper are old school.

———•———

Rocking chairs are old school.

———•———

Knitting is old school.

———•———

Shoveling snow is old school.

———•———

Raking leaves is old school.

Sewing machines are old school.

Cloth diapers are old school.

Wood-burning stoves
and fireplaces are old school.

John Muir was old school.

Rachel Carson was old school.

Sitting Bull was old school.

Roller skates are old school.

Scooters are old school.

———

Tree houses are old school.

———

Mending clothing and
darning socks are old school.

———

Repairing something instead
of throwing it out is old school.

———

Porch swings are old school.

———

Picnics are old school.

———

Homemade bread is old school.

———

Riding bikes is old school. In
the old school, parents hardly
ever drove their children anywhere.

12

OLD SCHOOL
PARENTS

In the old school, the parents raised the children and didn't let the children raise themselves. The antithesis of the old school is, "Let your children be who they are, but know where they are." In the old school, it was understood that children did not know how to behave or really have any idea who they were until their parents taught them how to behave and what kind of person to be. The old school believed that children would be better off if they were taught manners and taught to be useful.

In the old school, sex was for making babies. A girl wouldn't have sex with a boy unless she thought he was ready to get married and that he would help raise babies. Boys could hardly find anyone with whom to have sex unless they showed the good character to help raise babies and children.

In the old school, fewer than 1 percent of all children experienced the divorce of their parents.

Old School Parents

Family vacations to the
lake or beach are old school.

———

Having Thanksgiving dinner at your
grandparents' house is old school.

———

Showing family movies
on projectors is old school.

———

Camping is old school.

———

Having a set bedtime
as a child is old school.

———

Recognizing that a career of raising
children is more important than a
career of shuffling papers in an
office is old school.

———

Parents committed to
raising children is old school.

Reading to your children at bedtime is old school.

———

Old school parents teach their
children that the most courageous
thing to do is stand up for someone
who is being hurt or bullied.

———

Self-esteem in children is all right,
but humility in children is old school.

———

Camping out in your
backyard is old school.

———

Grandmothers and grandfathers
living in your house is old school.

———

Baby carriages are old school.

———

Teasing your brothers
or sisters is old school.

———•———

Weeding the garden, beating rugs, and
taking out trash are old school.

———•———

Teaching children with both rewards
and punishments is old school.

———•———

Telling your children to finish
their vegetables is old school.

———•———

Playing outside and then having
your mother or father scold
you for tracking dirt in
the house is old school.

———•———

Praying before you go to bed is old school.

13

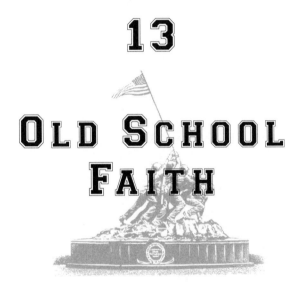

OLD SCHOOL
FAITH

*T*he old school understood the self-help value that went with practicing a religion. If you had troubles, an old school person would recommend you go to church. Religion teaches children to solve their own problems throughout their lives. Old school self-help therapy has the following principles:

God loves you just the way you are.

You should serve a higher purpose than your own self-centered interests.

Be kind to others.

Learn to delay gratification.

You are never alone, for God is always with you.

Learn a system of morality that serves as the framework for the thoughts and actions of your life.

Ask for help in prayer and bring troubles to God for advice and support.

You have spiritual support to face the greatest adversities and worst tragedies.

Learn the incomprehensible power of faith.

There is important meaning to life, and you should make your life mean something.

Old school religion teaches children how to face and overcome the most complicated of life's challenges. Religion is a lot less expensive than therapy.

In the old school, if you wanted to help disadvantaged people you majored in theology instead of sociology. You became a minister instead of a social worker. You nurtured their spirits and teleology rather than their material situation.

"OF ALL THE DISPOSITIONS AND HABITS WHICH LEAD TO POLITICAL PROSPERITY, RELIGION AND MORALITY ARE INDISPENSABLE SUPPORTS . . . AND LET US WITH CAUTION INDULGE THE SUPPOSITION, THAT MORALITY CAN BE MAINTAINED WITHOUT RELIGION."

—**George Washington**

Reading and studying the Book of Proverbs is old school.

Young, able-bodied people not
accepting handouts is old school.

———•———

Accepting phrases such as
"In God We Trust" as part of the
American fabric is old school.

———•———

Gandhi was old school.

———•———

Martin Luther King was old school.

———•———

Jesus is old school.

———•———

Joan of Arc was old school.

———•———

Confucius is old school.

Nuns are old school.

Mother Teresa was old school.

Making religion your
profession, as Gandhi, Rev. King, and
Mother Teresa did, is old school.

Political correctness
is not old school.

Observing the Sabbath and attending religious services at least once a week is old school.

———

14

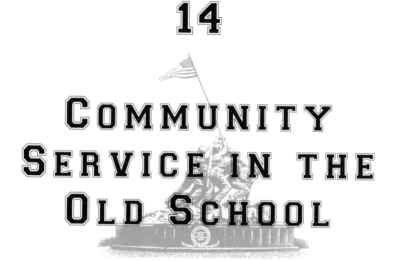

COMMUNITY
SERVICE IN THE
OLD SCHOOL

In the old school, there was not much talk about community service because being part of a community required what is now called "community service." You had to look after your kids so no one else would have to do it for you. In the old school, people often looked after their elderly relatives. The basic level of the community began with the family, and everyone was expected to take care of their families.

The old school community ethos was that you owed a life of service to your family, your neighborhood, and your country. The old school recognized the critical importance of being there for your family and neighbors every day for years.

The old school was powerful when service to others was called for by death, destruction, or hard times. Neighbors in old school neighborhoods understood the fundamental importance of helping neighbors in need.

The old school community ethos was more important for those who were the most needy. Low-income families and neighborhoods had to help each other more than any other families and neighborhoods. This is why during hard times, the old school has economic poverty but still a wealth of character.

In the old school, you took care of your family and you helped your neighbor because that's what a good American should do. Calling attention to it was considered the worst kind of conceit. Helping others for recognition or credit is the opposite of the old school community ethos.

"A government should not do for people what they ought to do for themselves," Abraham Lincoln said.

"THE NEW FRONTIER OF WHICH I SPEAK IS NOT A SET OF PROMISES—IT IS A SET OF CHALLENGES. IT SUMS UP NOT WHAT I INTEND TO OFFER THE AMERICAN PEOPLE, BUT WHAT I INTEND TO ASK OF THEM."

—John F. Kennedy

The New Frontier was old school.

A town commons is old school.

Naming streets, parks, and buildings
after war heroes is old school.

"Good fences make
good neighbors" is old school.

The Salvation Army is old school.

Shortcuts across
vacant lots are old school.

The way out of poverty in the old
school was hard work, education, or
enlisting in the armed services.

Granite or bronze
statues are old school.

———•———

Playgrounds are old school.

———•———

Cannons displayed in
town parks are old school.

———•———

The old school was clean. No
matter what your income
or situation in life, you could
keep yourself and your area clean.

———•———

Living and working in the same town
in which you grew up is old school.

———•———

Police athletic leagues and
church leagues are old school.

———•———

The best way to reduce crime in the old school was to expect that every family was connecting their children to a religious tradition.

Community Service in the Old School

Clean language is old school.

———

Potluck dinners are old school.

———

YMCAs and YWCAs
used to be old school.

———

Libraries and museums
are old school.

———

Shoveling your next-door
neighbor's sidewalk is old school.

———

Keeping things simple is old school.
The United States Constitution,
which guides the affairs of the
most technologically advanced
country in history, was written
on three and a half pages.

———

Going to your town fair is old school.

—·—

Military service is old school.

—·—

Marching in parades is old school.

—·—

Patriotism and sacrifice
for your country is old school.

—·—

Not many people were in
prisons in the old school.

—·—

VFW, Elks, and
Rotary are old school.

—·—

Armories turned into
gymnasiums are old school.

—·—

15

OLD SCHOOL MENTORING

The old school had a simple mentoring system. In the old school, every child automatically had two mentors assigned to them. Relatives, neighbors, and even public authorities expected the biological father and the biological mother to serve as mentors for any children created by an intimate relationship. There was no fund-raising campaign to pay the mentors, and there was no search for mentors. Everyone served as mentors to their own children.

The old school was first and foremost interested in right and wrong. There is not much moral diversity or ambivalence in the old school.

Hebrew school, catechism, and Sunday school are old school.

Being a good role model is old school.

Never making excuses is old school.

———

Never complaining is old school.

———

Narcissism is not old school.

———

Having childhood be organically connected to the process of growing into an adult is old school. Growing up in a way that connects the days and lessons of childhood to the admirable process of growing up into adults and parents is old school. Changing from children into a very different stage called "teenagers" and then trying to shift again to become responsible adults is not old school.

———

16

SPORTS IN THE OLD SCHOOL

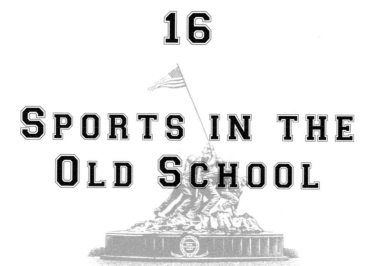

*O*ld school sports were based on the philosophy that "It's not whether you win or lose, but how you play the game." Athletes were taught that good character would lead to good athletic performances, which were measured in part by the score, and in part by the praise of coaches, and parents who recognized sportsmanship, hard work, courage, and honor as the highest goals of sports activities. Anyone who simply tried to excel in skill or victory was looked at as self-centered, shallow, and immature. Youth sports was conducted entirely at the local level, and only in high school did teams have moderate travel schedules.

"THE WORLD LOVES TALENT, BUT IT PAYS OFF ON CHARACTER."

—John Gardner

Neighborhood pick-up games are old school.

132

Bowling is old school, but bowling leagues are even more old school.

———

Playing a different sport each season is old school. In the old school, you only played the sports that were in season.

———

Amateur sports are old school.

———

The old school did not admire immature athletes no matter how good they were at sports. Anyone who was lazy, disrespectful to opponents, or disrespectful to officials was considered immature. Anyone who got in trouble with the law was immature.

———

The Olympics used to be old school.

———

The purpose of athletics in
the old school was to improve a
person's character by teaching
discipline, hard work, courage,
honor, and sportsmanship.

———

High school and college
marching bands are old school.

———

Playing Ping-Pong in a
friend's basement is old school.

———

Giving the ball back to the referee
after a touchdown is old school.

———

Sports in the Old School

The organ at baseball
games is old school.

———

Humble athletes are old school.

———

Quarterbacks calling
their own plays is old school.

———

Roy Campanella was old school.

———

Joe DiMaggio was old school.

———

Listening to the game
on the radio is old school.

———

Gordie Howe is old school.

———

Bobby Orr is old school.

Fenway Park is old school.

Wrigley Field is old school.

Martial arts are old school.

Natural grass is old school.

Cinder tracks are old school.

Doubleheaders are old school.

Baseball is old school.

Ice-skating on frozen
ponds is old school.

Playing golf using
a caddie is old school.

———•———

Carrying your own golf bag
is also old school.

———•———

David Robinson, Brooks Robinson,
Eddie Robinson, and Jackie
Robinson are all old school.

———•———

Wyomia Tyus is old school.

———•———

Tom Landry was old school.

———•———

Dick Butkus, Johnny Unitas, and Vince Lombardi are all old school.

Joe Paterno is old school.

———

Bear Bryant was old school.

———

John Wooden is old school.

———

Joe Louis was old school.

———

Watching the fights on
Saturday night is old school.

———

Banked wooden indoor
tracks are old school.

———

In the old
school, people
got a stick
of gum with
their pack of
baseball cards.

Coaches who don't argue
with referees are old school.

———

Street hockey is old school.

———

Croquet is old school.

———

Jump rope is old school.

———

Button-up baseball uniforms
with high stirrups are old school.

———

Touch football is old school.

———

Catching fly balls in baseball with two hands is old school.

The basket catch made famous
by Willie Mays is old school.

—•—

Outfielders throwing out
base runners without the help
of a cut-off man are old school.

—•—

Straight-on place-kickers
are old school.

—•—

Cal Ripken Jr. is old school.

—•—

Ernie Banks is old school.

—•—

Bob Cousy and Bill Russell
are old school.

—•—

Sports in the Old School

Wind sprints are old school.

———

Jumping jacks are old school.

———

Push-ups, sit-ups,
and chin-ups are old school.

———

Sporting events without
title sponsors are old school.

———

Rope tows on ski
slopes are old school.

———

Toboggans, sleds, and
flying saucers on freshly
fallen snow are old school.

———

Soapbox derby races are old school.

Sports in the Old School

Fishing is old school.

Snowball fights, snowmen,
and snow forts are old school.

—•—

Tackling dummies and
blocking sleds are old school.

—•—

Badminton is old school.

—•—

Basketball referees
calling three-second and
traveling violations are old school.

—•—

Swimming holes are old school.

—•—

Shirts and skins is old school.

—•—

Persimmon wood golf
clubs are old school.

—•—

EPILOGUE

The old school wasn't perfect. It had flaws. But the old school was engaged in a never-ending search for the truth. The search was carried on primarily in churches and schools, but also in labs and libraries. Many people in the old school smoked cigarettes. But old school scientists discovered that smoking was deadly. Millions of smokers who thought they were doing the right thing suddenly found themselves doing wrong.

For a while, the old school believed in racism, but in sermons and classes we learned that all men are created equal. Then, for awhile, the old school believed in segregation. But in more sermons and more classes we came to understand that the civil rights movement contained the wisdom of the ages, and it was an old school movement.